THE WORLD'S SILLIEST KIDS' JOKES

THE WORLD'S SILLIEST KIDS' JOKES

So silly you'll laugh your pants off!

Kay Barnham

ARCTURUS

ARCTURUS

This edition published in 2010 by Arcturus Publishing Limited
26/27 Bickels Yard, 151–153 Bermondsey Street,
London SE1 3HA

ISBN: 978-1-84837-496-6
CH001395EN

Author: Kay Barnham
Illustrator: David Mostyn
Editor: Kate Overy
Design and layout: Gary Sutherland

Printed in Singapore

CONTENTS

CHAPTER 1
SILLY SPOOKS

What do dirty monsters drink on hot summer days?
Slime cordial.

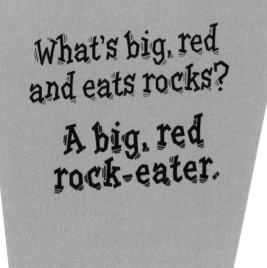

What's big, red and eats rocks?

A big, red rock-eater.

What happens when a dirty, stinky green monster goes paddling in the Red Sea?

It gets wet.

Why did the weather witch put her wand in the microwave?

She wanted to cast a warm spell.

What did the ghost say to his girlfriend?

You look boo-tiful in the moonlight!

What do dirty monsters eat on hot summer days?

Lice lollies.

Did you hear about the police officers who kept watch on the vampire's castle all night?

It was a stake out.

Q. What do you call a ghost who haunts the town hall?

A. A night mayor.

SILLY SPOOKS

What's as sharp and pointy as one of Dracula's fangs?

His other fang.

Did you hear about the angry coffin?
It flipped its lid.

What do you give a seasick monster?
Plenty of room.

Why did the cannibal prefer to live alone?

He was totally fed up with other people.

What's evil on the inside and purple on the outside?

A witch dressed as an aubergine.

What was the elephant witch doctor called?
Mumbo Jumbo.

Did you hear about the monster comedian?
He was horribly funny.

Why did the ghoul take his suitcase to the funfair?
He wanted to catch the ghost train.

FUNFAIR

SILLY SPOOKS

What do you call a monster in an aeroplane seat? Stuck.

How many vampires does it take to screw in a lightbulb?

None. They like the dark.

Why did the Egyptian mummy call the doctor? Because of the coffin!

What type of coat does a witch wear in the rain?

A wet one.

There were two apples bobbing in a bucket of water on Halloween.

One said, 'Crikey, this water's cold.' The other said, 'Aaaaargh! A talking apple!'

What did the ghostly commentator use at the Ghouls' Sports Day?

A loudspooker.

How did the doctor bring the ghost back to life? He took it into the living room.

What do birds sing at Halloween?

Trick or tweet.

SILLY SPOOKS

What spooker player are footballers most afraid of?

The grim keeper.

How do you rid a haunted house of ghosts and ghouls?

With scare freshener.

Did you hear about the little ghost with glasses who couldn't scare anyone, no matter how hard he tried?

He was short-frighted.

What type of mistakes do ghosts make?

Boo-boos.

How do you greet a two-headed monster?

Hello hello!

What's a ghoul's favourite meal?

Spookhetti bolognese.

What do ghosts watch at the haunted theatre?

Romeo and Ghoulliet.

What did the ghostly footballer shout when he scored?

Ghoul!

SILLY SPOOKS

Did you hear about the
fisherman who saw a spook?

It was the ghostguard.

What do witches do
when they stay in
hotels?

They order
broom service.

What did the ghostly teacher
say to his puzzled pupils?
Watch the board and I'll
go through it again.

Did you hear about the
musical ghost?

He wrote haunting melodies.

How do you lock a graveyard at night?

With a skeleton key.

How did the famous ghost publish his life story after he was dead?

It was ghost written.

How do vampires get washed?

In a bloodbath.

Q. What do monsters eat on hot, sunny days?

A. Eyes cream.

SiLLY SPOOKS

Which is a ghoul's favourite day of the week?

Moanday.

Which is a cannibal's favourite day of the week?

Chewsday.

Which is a spider's favourite day of the week?

Websday.

Which is a vampire's favourite day of the week?

Thirstday.

Which is a ghost's favourite day of the week?

Frightday.

Which is a poltergeist's favourite day of the week?

Scatterday.

Which is a dirty monster's favourite day of the week?

Scumday.

SILLY SPOOKS

What's a banshee's favourite animal?

The whale.

How do ghosts travel on holiday?

In a scareoplane.

Why do witches never need dictionaries?

Because they're brilliant spellers.

How does a monster with five heads pick his noses?

One at a time.

What do you get if you cross Tinkerbell with a werewolf?

A hairy fairy.

What do you call a werewolf who's spent his life's savings?

Paw.

What pudding do banshees eat at Wimbledon?

Strawberries and scream.

What do banshees take on holiday?

Sun scream.

SILLY SPOOKS

Where do
witches fly?

**In the
atmosfear.**

How did the wizard
tell the time?

**He checked his
wrist witch.**

Why do witches ride
broomsticks?

**Vacuum cleaners
are too heavy.**

Why do witches eat bacon sandwiches?

They love the cackling.

How did the punk wizard spike his hair?

He used scare gel.

Why didn't the wizard use a pencil to write down his spells?

There was no point.

What's a spook's favourite sweet treat?

Shockolate.

Did you hear about the poltergeist who haunted the china shop?

He was smashing.

SILLY SPOOKS

What kind of pet does a witch have?

A scaredy cat.

Did you hear about the hairy beast swimming down the rapids?

It was a weir wolf.

What game do banshees play at parties?

Hide and shriek.

Which is a ghost's favourite ice cream?

Boo-berry.

What do vampires drink?

Decoffinated coffee.

Which is a vampire's favourite ice cream?
Veinilla.

What type of music do ghosts like to dance to?
Haunted house music.

What do Egyptian mummies dance to?
Wrap music.

SiLLY SPOOKS

What do baby ghosts play? Peekaboo!

What do you call a haunted detective story? A whoooooooodunnit.

Q. Did you hear about the ghostly horse that galloped at midnight?

A. She was a nightmare.

What do ghosts say before they begin a meal?
Bone appetite!

What do you say to a vampire when he gets married?
Coagulations!

Where do witches keep their bits and bobs?
In hag bags.

What do ghosts take everywhere with them?
Mobile groans.

What is Count Dracula's favourite tourist attraction?
The Vampire State Building.

25

SILLY SPOOKS

Which is a ghost's favourite type of puzzle?

A cryptic crossword.

Who wrote the play about the haunted church?

The crypt writer.

Where did the banshee look up telephone numbers?

In the Yeller Pages.

What do vampires play when it's raining?

Stakes and ladders.

Did you hear about the vampire who went to the fast-food restaurant?

He wanted a quick bite.

What do ghosts wear when they drive anywhere?

A sheetbelt.

What do French ghosts say in the morning?

Bone-jour.

What do you call a vampire who falls for practical jokes?

Sucker!

SILLY SPOOKS

Did you hear about the well-behaved witch's cat?

It was purrfect.

What did the vampire think of his new false teeth?

They were fangtastic!

Q. Did you hear about the identical twin witches?

A. No one could tell which witch was which.

What do vampires sing
on New Year's Eve?
Auld Fang Syne.

How do monsters
sign their letters?
Best vicious.

What do vampires
do for their summer
holidays?
They go vamping.

How does a witch
feel after long,
bumpy journeys?
Broom sick.

R.I.P

Why don't mummies
ever take a break?
**Because they
never want
to unwind.**

STRAWBERRIES AND SCREAM

One dark night, Count Dracula is prowling outside a wedding party when he hears a whistling noise and then ... **SPLAT!** A sausage roll catches him on the chin and knocks him backwards. 'Ooof!' he says. 'I wasn't expecting that.'

He continues on his way, looking for unsuspecting victims with lovely necks when ... **BLAT, BLAT!** Two mushroom vol-au-vents hit him, one after the other, messing up his slicked-back black hair. 'What's going on?' he mutters, just

before a deluge of yummy missiles heads his way. **KER-SPLAT! SPLOSH! BAM! WHAM!** SPLOOSH! Cheese straws, fairy cakes, vegetable samosas, sandwiches, ice-cream sundaes and finally a huge bowl of sherry trifle

bombard him. His scary black cape is covered, his legendary cool is destroyed and his teeth are dripping with strawberry sauce.

Dracula is not looking good and he's feeling terrible. Then suddenly, the truth dawns on him ... 'I know who's behind this!' he cries. 'It's Buffet the Vampire Slayer!'

CHAPTER 2
ICKY STICKY

What's the whiffiest country in the world?

Phew Zealand.

What's the whiffiest city in the world?

Hong Pong.

What's the stickiest and sweetest type of tree?

A tree-cle.

Q. Why did the two-week-old bottle of milk vanish?

A. It had gone off.

Q: WHAT DID ONE SMELLY SHEEP SAY TO THE OTHER SMELLY SHEEP?

What's the ickiest ice cream flavour?

Lemon and slime.

What's loud, sticky and made of phlegm?

A cough sweet.

Did you hear about the eggs who kept throwing themselves at unsuspecting pupils?

They were practical yolkers.

What did the chewing gum say to the shoe?

I'm stuck on you.

Why do bees have icky, sticky hair?

They use honeycombs.

ICKY STICKY

What did the cannibals do after the wedding speeches?

They toasted the bride and groom.

What's really icky, really stinky and visits Earth every 76 years?

Halley's vomit.

Did you hear about the American bear who tripped and fell into a blender?

It was a grizzly accident.

What do you get if you boil up 25 cars, three buses and a lorry load of sugar?

Traffic jam.

What do you call a boy standing in the middle of a squishy cowpat?

An in-cow-poop.

What did the Dutch pet-shop owner spread on his croissant?

Hamster jam.

What did the stinky skunk with the terrible memory say when the wind changed direction?

It's all coming back to me now.

ICKY STICKY

What did one egg say to the other egg when it told a joke?

You crack me up.

What type of blood does a pessimist have?

B Negative.

What steps should you take if there's an invasion of giant nose-picking monsters?

Great big ones.

Why did the girl pick her nose at school?

Because she wasn't allowed to pick it at home.

Why did the amoeba cross the microscope?

To get to the other slide.

What are big, nutritious and fly together at breakneck speed?

The Red Marrows.

If you divided a treacle tart in half, then in half again and then you divided each piece into 24 pieces, what would you get?

Really sticky fingers.

ICKY STICKY

Why did the clown throw mud pies at the audience?

It was jest for laughs.

What's a monster's favourite dessert?

Lice pudding.

What's green and has four legs and a trunk?

A seasick elephant.

Why don't cannibals eat clowns?

Because they taste funny.

Why was the killer whale sick after gobbling up the vicar?

Because it's hard to keep a good man down.

Why is cutting a huge, creamy slice of Black Forest Gateau the easiest job in the world?

It's a piece of cake.

What was the fly doing in the gravy? The breaststroke.

Q. Why did the handyman have to get false teeth?

A. Because he kept biting his nails.

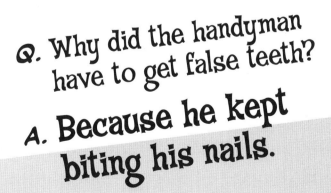

ICKY STICKY

Q. What did the duck say to the beautician when she bought lip gloss?

A. Put it on my bill, please.

Why did the hedgehog cross the road?

To show its guts.

What do you say to a monster with a really runny nose?

Goo away!

Why did the pig go to the amusement arcade?

He wanted to play the slop machine.

What did the monster barman put in all the drinks?

Lice and a slice.

What type of umbrella does a stinky, sweaty monster use on a rainy day?

A wet one.

What's the stinkiest letter of the alphabet?

Ewwwwwwwww.

What do you call a boy with his head down the toilet?

Huey.

ICKY STICKY

What did the speedy squashed tomato say to the slow squashed tomato?

Ketchup!

Why did the beauty contest winner put petit pois in the blender?

She wanted whirled peas.

Q. Did you hear about the upside-down man?

A. His feet smell and his nose runs.

How many bites can you take out of a whole jam sandwich?

Just the one. Then it's no longer a whole jam sandwich!

What is the most cultured pudding in the world?

Yoghurt.

What do cats like to eat in the summer?

Mice cream.

Did you hear about the poorly computer? It had a nasty virus.

iCKY STiCKY

Why was the pig covered in ink?

Because it had just come back from the pen.

What do cannibals call athletes?

Fast-food.

Why couldn't Batman go fishing?

Because Robin had eaten all the worms.

What did the monster say when he was served a particularly squishy, wriggly maggot?

Delicious grub.

What's a spider's favourite meal?

Corn on the cobweb.

What's yellow and meows?

Pus.

What's the difference between dogs and fleas?

Dogs can have fleas, but fleas can't have dogs.

What did one slug say to the other?

Slime flies when you're having fun.

ICKY STICKY

How do you make
a frog float?

...ice cream
and a bottle
of lemonade.
Cheers!

What's brown
and sounds
like a bell?

Dung!

What's red
and silly?

A blood
clot.

What do you get if
you drop an elephant
on a baby butterfly?

A splatterpillar!

Q: WHAT DID THE SNAIL CALL HIS HOUSE?

What was the snail doing on the M6?
About 20 millimetres an hour.

Why are snails' shells so shiny?
They use snail varnish.

Why didn't the nose want to go to school?
Because he was always getting picked on.

Q. What do you call a multi-storey pigpen?
A. A styscraper.

ICKY STICKY

Did you hear about the fly that flew into the sieve at top speed?

It was another fine mesh he'd got himself into.

What's the difference between bogeys and Brussels sprouts?

Children won't eat Brussels sprouts.

What are a hamster's favourite biscuits?

Hammy dodgers.

What did the snail say when he'd climbed onto the tortoise's shell?

Wheeeeeeee!

What do you give a horse with a tickly throat?

Cough stirrup.

What's the stinkiest animal in the world?

A kangapoo.

A: MICHELLE!

Why are the soles of elephants' feet yellow?

So they can lie upside down and hide in a bowl of custard.

Have you ever found an elephant in your bowl of custard?

No? Well, the yellow feet must do the trick, then.

iCKY STiCKY

What's sweet, sticky and goes swinging through the jungle?

Tarzipan.

What colour is poop?

Poople.

What goes green, red, green, red, green, red?

A toad in a blender.

What's green, slightly stinky and has a trunk?

A seasick holidaymaker.

What's an ogre's favourite colour?

Slime green.

How do you make
a teddy bear
go woof?

**Put it on a
bonfire.**

What do you get if you cross
an owl with a sewer rat?

A bird that stinks but
doesn't give two hoots.

Did you hear about
the chicken that
told dirty jokes?

It was foul.

DESSERT IN THE DESERT

A family goes on an adventure holiday in the desert. They're having a great time, experiencing new things every day.

One day, they meet a grumpy old camel, who frowns at them all and then spits. 'How rude!' says Mum. But Dad laughs it off. 'That sort of thing happens all the time in the desert,' he says. 'It's totally normal.'

The next day, the son and daughter spot a group of palm trees in the distance. The family trudges across the dry sand towards it. 'How strange to find trees in the desert!' says the son. But Dad laughs it off. 'That's an oasis,' he says. 'You find them all over the desert. It's totally normal.'

The following day, the family reaches a town. There, they find a lively and colourful market. The smells are delicious and everyone is looking forward to a hearty meal. 'We'll have some typical regional food,' says Dad knowledgeably. He asks for meat and vegetables at the first stall they come to. 'Sorry,' says the stall holder. 'I've only got sherry trifle. There's no meat or veg here.' Dad looks disappointed. 'Oh,' he says.

At the next stall, Dad asks again. 'I'd like your best savoury regional speciality,' he says. 'Sorry, mate,' replies the stall holder. 'I've got banana and chocolate trifle, but that's it.' Dad frowns. 'Oh,' he says. And at every single stall they visit, the answer is the same.

They all sell gloriously sticky trifles – blueberry trifle, strawberry trifle and orange trifle, but no meat and no veg. Eventually, the family leaves.

'And I suppose that's totally normal too?' says Mum. 'No,' replies Dad. 'That's a trifle bazaar.'

CHAPTER 3
COMEDY CREATURES

Why did it take the Dalmatian so long to choose a holiday?

He was looking for just the right spot.

Did you hear about the spiders who got married?

They had a huge webbing.

What kind of bird steals from the rich and gives to the poor?

Robin Hood.

Where do penguins vote?

At the South Poll.

Where do pigs park their cars?

In a car pork.

Why did the partridge and the pheasant dress up as clowns?

They were game for a laugh.

What made the fly fly?

The spider spied her.

What happened when the frog's car broke down?

It was toad away.

COMEDY CREATURES

How do birds see what's behind them?

They look in their wing mirrors.

How did the bumblebee contact his friend?

He gave him a buzz.

Why do sheep have woolly coats? Anoraks don't suit them.

Where are elephants found?

They're so huge, it's quite difficult to lose them in the first place.

Did you hear about the cross pig that lost its voice from oinking too much?

It was disgruntled.

What is a fish's favourite type of music?

Bubble rap.

Why do fish live in salty water?

Pepper makes them sneeze.

Where do giraffes go for their lessons?

High school.

$$10 \times \frac{9^3}{x} = \sqrt{\frac{29}{x+6a}}$$

$$=$$

COMEDY CREATURES

What do you get if you put a mouse in the washing machine?

Squeaky-clean clothes.

What has feathers and writes?

A ballpoint hen.

What do lizards put on their bathroom walls?

Rep-tiles.

BLEEP!

Q. Where do you buy baby birds?

A. At the chickout.

A black horse walks into a pub called The Black Horse. 'Hi!' says the barman. 'Did you know that this pub was named after you?'

'Really?' says the horse. 'The pub's called Eric?'

How do scientists know that carrots are excellent for eyesight?

Because you never see a rabbit wearing spectacles.

What's the worst kind of cat?

A catastrophe!

What did the celebrity squirrels sign before they got married?

A pre-nutshell agreement.

COMEDY CREATURES

How do you stop
a dog from barking
in the back seat of a car?
Put it in the front seat.

What do you
do with a blue
parrot?

Try to cheer
it up.

Two chickens
walked into a
building the
other day.

You would
have thought
at least one
of them
would
have
seen it.

What do you get
if you cross an insect
and a rabbit?

Bugs Bunny.

Why don't Arctic foxes eat penguins?

They can't get the wrappers off.

What is a rabbit's favourite type of dancing?

Hip hop.

What do cats watch on television in the evening?

The Six O' Clock Mews.

Q. What do penguins do in their spare time?

A. They chill.

COMEDY CREATURES

What noise do porcupines make when they kiss?

Owwwww!

How do rabbits keep their fur tidy?

With hare-spray.

What do you call a donkey with three legs?

A wonkey.

What's brown, furry and has twelve paws?

The Three Bears.

Did you hear about the horse that had six legs?

It had forelegs at the front and two legs at the back.

Why did the Wild West dog limp into the Wild West town?

He came to find the cowboy who shot his paw!

What do birds watch on television?

The feather forecast.

What did the chimpanzee do when he saw a sign saying, 'Wet floor'?

He threw water on it.

COMEDY CREATURES

How do you catch a
totally unique rabbit?

Unique up on it!

How do you catch a
tame rabbit?

The tame way.
Unique up on it.

Why do Dalmatians
never play hide-and-seek?

They are
always spotted.

Q. What kind of furry
animal likes to live
underwater?

A. The Octo-pussy!

What do cats drink in the desert?

Evaporated milk.

Why does a cow moo? Because its horns don't work.

How do you catch a squirrel?

Climb up a tree and act like a nut.

Why did the cat become a nurse?

She wanted to be a first-aid kit.

COMEDY CREATURES

What's big, furry and flies?

A hot-air baboon.

What's the most difficult key to turn?

A donkey.

How do you stop moles digging up your garden?

Hide the spades.

What happens when ducks fly backwards?

They quack up.

What's the difference between a crazy rabbit and a forged bank note?

One's a mad bunny and the other's bad money.

What do you call a horse that likes cross-stitch and stamp-collecting?

A hobby horse.

How do cows keep up with current affairs?

They watch the Ten O' Clock Moos.

What type of bird digs underground?

A mynah bird.

COMEDY CREATURES

What sea creatures do you find on legal documents?

Seals.

What do sharks eat at birthday parties?

Ice cream and jellyfish.

Where do tadpoles change into frogs?

In a croakroom.

Why should you never trust a whale with your deepest, darkest secrets?

Because they're all blubbermouths.

Which fish plays an instrument?

The sea-bass.

What's grey, has four legs and a trunk?

A mouse going on holiday.

Which football team came top of the Animal League?

The hedgehogs.
They won on points.

What type of biscuits do birds love?

Chocolate-chirrup.

COMEDY CREATURES

Which birds are cricketers really scared of?

Ducks.

How do you catch a purple elephant?

In a purple-elephant trap.

How do you catch a green elephant?

Paint it purple and then catch it in a purple-elephant trap.

Where do camels keep their money?

In sand banks.

What do you call a young goat that learns martial arts?

The Karate Kid.

Why did the silly boy oil the mice?

Because they squeaked.

Where do beavers keep their money?

In river banks.

How do you hire a horse?

Put a brick under each hoof.

COMEDY CREATURES

Why wasn't the butterfly invited to the dance?

Because it was a mothball.

Did you hear about the Christmas turkey who tried to escape the roasting pan?

He was foiled.

What is grey, goes bzzzzzzzz and loves to nibble cheese?

A mousequito!

Did you hear about the well-behaved cat?

It was purrfect.

What's the untidiest insect? The litterbug.

What goes dash-dash-squeak, dash-dash-squeak, dot-dot-dash-squeak, dot-dot-dot-squeak, dot-squeak?

Mouse code.

Did you hear about the little cat sanctuary where poor, abandoned cats go to live?

It was tiny. You couldn't swing a cat in there!

What do rhinoceroses have that no other animal has?

Baby rhinoceroses.

COMEDY CREATURES

What do dinosaurs rest their teacups on?

Tyrannosaucers.

What do you call a herd of cows with a sense of humour?

Laughing stock.

What's grey and bounces?

An elephant on a trampoline.

What do you get if you cross an angry sheep with a cross cow?

An animal that's in a baaaaaaaaaaaaaaaad moooooooooooooood.

Why is a hedgehog the most selfish creature in the countryside?

It refuses to share the hedge.

Pretend that you're teetering on top of a towering cliff and a herd of rampaging elephants are thundering towards you. What should you do?

Stop pretending.

Q. What has two humps and is found at the South Pole?

A. A lost camel.

SOOTH POLE

Where do turtles go when it rains?

To a shell-ter.

COMEDY CREATURES

Q. Which animal never goes to the hairdresser?

A. A bald eagle.

How do you get an elephant into the fridge?

Open the door, shove him in and then shut the door.

What do you get if you cross a porcupine and a giraffe?

A very tall toothbrush.

How do you get a rhino into the fridge?

Open the door, pull out the elephant, shove in the rhino and then shut the door.

Which is the chattiest animal?

A yak.

What do camels wear when they play hide-and-seek?

Camel-flage.

How can you tell which end of a worm is its head?

Tell it a silly joke and see which end laughs.

What did the cheetah say to her cubs when she was teaching them to hunt?

Never step onto the road unless you see a zebra crossing.

COMEDY CREATURES

Q. What do you call a singing lizard with a great sense of rhythm?

A. A rap-tile.

What's the sweetest insect?
A humbug.

Why did Bo Peep lose her sheep?

She had a crook with her.

What do flies wear on their feet?

Shoos.

What did the Cinderella fish wear to the ball?

A glass flipper!

Which insect is terrific at sums?

An account-ant.

Why was the cat scared of the tree?

Because of its bark.

What does a cat sleep on?

A caterpillow.

HIDDEN TALENT

A badly dressed, downtrodden man walks into a café and orders a cup of coffee.

'Sure', says the waitress, 'But I need the money first, you look like you're broke!'

The man answers, 'You're right. I haven't got a penny, but if I show you something amazing will you give me a cup?'

'It's a deal', says the waitress, intrigued.

So the man reaches into the pocket of his tatty coat and pulls out a mouse. He places the mouse on the counter and hands it a tiny guitar. Immediately the mouse begins to play the teeny tiny guitar with ease, strumming away like a rock star.

'Wow!' says the waitress, 'That was amazing, I've never seen anything like it! Here's your free coffee.'

The man drinks his coffee and the little mouse disappears back into his coat pocket.

'I'll have another', says the man.

'Well, you know the deal,' replies the waitress, 'Show me another trick and your coffee's on the house!'

The man shrugs his shoulders and reaches into his pocket again. This time he pulls out a frog. He places the frog on the counter and immediately it begins to sing. And what glorious singing! The whole café stops to listen to the tiny frog with the big voice.

Suddenly a stranger approaches the scruffy man and says 'Hey, how much for the singing frog? I'll give you 200 for him!'

'Sure, he's yours.' says the man.

The stranger picks up the frog from the counter, hands over the cash, and skips out of the café, not believing his luck.

'Are you crazy?' says the waitress, 'You sold your singing frog for 200, but you could have got millions! He could have made you a fortune!'

'Actually, he's not worth anything, says the man. 'The mouse is a great ventriloquist.'

CHAPTER 4
GIGGLES AND GROANS

Why didn't the skeleton cross the road?

He didn't have the guts.

Why didn't the banana snore?

He didn't want to wake up the rest of the bunch!

Q. Doctor, doctor, I think I'm a caterpillar.

A. Don't worry. You'll soon change.

Doctor, doctor,
I feel like a python.
You can't get round
me just like that!

Knock knock.
Who's there?
Norma Lee.
Norma Lee who?
Norma Lee I'd
ring the doorbell.

Knock knock.
Who's there?
Halle.
Halle who?
Hallelujah!
I'm here
to sing
Christmas
carols!

What do you call
a man who's made
of newspaper?
Russell.

Doctor, doctor,
I think I'm a nit.
Just get out
of my hair!

GIGGLES AND GROANS

What do you call a woman who takes people to court?
Sue.

Knock knock.
Who's there?
Anna.
Anna who?
Anna one, anna two ...

How many police officers does it take to screw in a lightbulb?
None. It turns itself in.

Doctor, doctor, I think I'm a frog.
So what's the problem?
I'm sure I'm going to croak.

Doctor, doctor, I feel like a mosquito.
Buzz off!

Doctor, doctor,
I keep thinking
I'm a woodworm.

**That must be so
boring for you.**

Knock knock.
Who's there?
Toodle.
Toodle who?
You're going
already?

What do you
get if you cross
a painter with a
police officer?

A brush with
the law.

GIGGLES AND GROANS

Why did the cockerel cross the road?

To prove that he wasn't a chicken!

Doctor, doctor, I've got flat feet.

Here's a bicycle pump to blow them up again.

Doctor, doctor, I think I'm a cow.

Pull the udder one.

BILL

What do you call a woman who sets fire to all her bills?

Bernadette.

Doctor, doctor, I'm sorry I'm late for my appointment, but I sprained my ankle.

That's a lame excuse!

Knock knock.
Who's there?
Eve.
Eve who?
Eve-ning!

Doctor, doctor, I just swallowed a sheep!
How do you feel?
Baaaaaaaaad.

Doctor, doctor, I've lost my memory!
When did this happen?
When did what happen?

GIGGLES AND GROANS

Knock knock.

Who's there?

Maia.

Maia who?

Maia totally pooped marathon-runner have a sit down, please?

What do you call a man who keeps you fit? Jim!

Doctor, doctor, I can't stop pulling funny faces.

What's wrong with that?

The people with funny faces are getting fed up with me.

Doctor, doctor, you've removed my tonsils, my adenoids and my appendix, but I still feel ill.

That's quite enough out of you.

Knock knock.
Who's there?
Eva.
Eva who?
Eva fancied
double glazing?

How many amoebas
does it take to
change a lightbulb?
One. No, two!
No, four! No,
eight ... sixteen ...
thirty-two!

Why did the
Roman chicken
cross the road?
She was worried
that someone
would Caesar.

What do you call a
bad-tempered bee?
A grumblebee.

GIGGLES AND GROANS

Doctor, doctor,
I feel flushed.

You must have flu.

No, I walked here.

Where did the police officer live?
999 Letsby Avenue.

Doctor, doctor,
can you give me something
for my kidneys?

Yes, here's half a
pound of steak.

Knock knock.

Who's there?

Scott.

Scott who?

Scott nothing
to do with you.

What do you get
if you cross a sheep
with a bucket
of water?

A wet blanket.

What do you call a man with a car number plate on the back of his head?
Reg.

Knock knock.

Who's there?

Twit too.

Twit too who?

That's a fantastic owl impression!

Doctor, doctor, I have asparagus sprouting from my ears.

How did that happen?

I've no idea. I planted beetroot.

GIGGLES AND GROANS

Knock knock.
Who's there?
Claudette.
Claudette who?
Claudette all
of my chocolate!

Doctor, doctor,
I keep thinking
I'm Mozart.

I'll be with you
in a minuet.

Why did the
cow cross
the road?

To get to the
udder side.

Knock knock.
Who's there?
Lydia.
Lydia who?
Lydia teapot
looks a bit loose.
Shall I fix it?

Doctor, doctor,
I'm not very tall.
You'll just
have to be a
little patient.

Why did the second cow cross the road?

To get to the moo-vies.

Why do ducks eat biscuits?

Because they're quackers!

Doctor, doctor, my throat is very sore.

Open that window and stick your tongue out.

Will that make me feel better?

No. I can't stand my next-door neighbour.

GIGGLES AND GROANS

What do you call a man who pickles himself in salty water?

Brian.

Doctor, doctor, I've got an urge to hang dangerously from the window ledge!

Hold on a minute.

Doctor, doctor, I'm allergic to the high jump.

Don't worry, you'll soon get over it!

Knock knock.

Who's there?

Hugh.

Hugh who?

Hugh d'you think it is!

Doctor, doctor, I'm addicted to fishing.

When you're feeling better, drop me a line.

How many librarians does it take to change a lightbulb?

Two. One to screw it in and one to say, 'Shhhhhh!' at the squeaking noise.

What do you call a man who squeezes through your letterbox?

Bill.

Q. How many magicians does it take to change a lightbulb?

A. It depends what you'd like to change it into!

GIGGLES AND GROANS

Man One:
My wife's gone
on holiday.

Man Two: Jamaica?

Man One:
No, she went of
her own accord.

Doctor, doctor,
I can't do this
crossword!
What's wrong?
I haven't a clue.

Man Two: My wife's gone
on holiday too.
Man One: Jakarta?
Man Two: No, she flew.

Doctor, doctor,
I feel like
a cup of tea.
So do I. Make
me one while
you're at it.

Doctor, doctor,
I feel like a bowl
of custard.
Sit down and
don't be
so thick.

Why did the shaggy
sheep cross the road?
To get to the
baa baa shop.

How many aerospace engineers
does it change to change a lightbulb?
None.
It's not rocket science!

What do you call
a man who's good at
fixing things?
Andy.

GIGGLES AND GROANS

What do you call a woman who likes to help old people with their shopping?

Carrie.

Knock knock.
Who's there?
Justin.
Justin who?
Justin time for dinner!

Doctor, doctor, I keep thinking I'm a chicken.
Get stuffed!

What do you call a man who wins every race he enters?

Victor.

Why did the elastic chicken cross the road?

She wanted to stretch her legs.

Doctor, doctor, I feel like a snooker player.

You're going to pot.

Constantinople is a very long word. Can you spell it?

C, O, N, S, T, A, N, T, I, N, O, P, L, E.

Don't be silly! It is spelt like this ... I, T!

Doctor, doctor, my eyesight's getting worse.

I'll say it is. This is the library.

GIGGLES AND GROANS

Doctor, doctor, I think I'm a bungee jumper! You've probably been a bit up and down lately.

Doctor, doctor, my legs feel like jelly. **Don't worry. They'll be better in a trifle.**

What do you call a woman who does impressions of emergency vehicles?

Nina.

What do you get if you cross a honeydew and a sheepdog?

A melon collie.

Knock knock.

Who's there?

Isobel.

Isobel who?

Isobel really necessary when you have such a great door knocker?

What do you call a woman with a nut tree on her head?

Hazel.

What do you call a man who can't help pinching things?

Nick.

Q. What do you call a woman with a cat on her head?

A. Kitty.

GIGGLES AND GROANS

What do you call a man with
a road map on his head?

Miles.

What do you call
a really tiny
woman?

Dot.

What do you
call a man with
three raincoats?

Max.

How did the chicken get
to the other side without
being squashed?

It was clucky.

One.

How many fortune tellers does it take to change a lightbulb?

Doctor, doctor, I just swallowed plutonium!

Hmm. You may get atomic ache.

Q. What do you call a man with an oversized raincoat?

A. Big Mac.

Doctor, doctor, I keep thinking I'm an alarm clock.

I'll see you in a tick.

GIGGLES AND GROANS

Why did the pig cross the road really, really slowly?

Because it was a road hog.

How do you get an idiot to laugh at the end of the day?

Tell him a joke at the start of the day.

Knock knock.
Who's there? Anya.
Anya who?
Anya best behaviour, please!

Why did the chewing gum cross the road?

Because it was stuck to the chicken's foot.

Doctor, doctor, I keep thinking I'm a stand-up comedian.

You must be joking.

Why do monkeys swing in trees? Because there aren't any swings in the jungle.

What did one wall say to the other wall? I'll meet you at the corner.

Knock knock.

Who's there?

Barbara.

Barbara who?

Barbara black sheep, have you any wool?

A BIG LET DOWN

The inflatable boy went to an inflatable school and had his lessons in an inflatable classroom, with his inflatable friends. He had an inflatable teacher, who spouted a lot of hot air during lessons, but otherwise told the inflatable boy lots of very useful facts.

One unfortunate day, the inflatable boy was pinning up a poster on the non-inflatable noticeboard. But he slipped and punctured the wall of the classroom. Slowly, and with a great hisssssss, the room began to deflate. The inflatable teacher rushed over to take the drawing pin off the boy, but there was a loud 'pop' and he began to deflate.

There was once an inflatable boy who lived in an inflatable world. He had an inflatable mum and an inflatable dad, who puffed up with pride whenever they saw him.

'Oh no!' cried the inflatable boy. He grabbed the pin back, but in the process accidentally pricked his finger. Hisssssss. He began to deflate too!

After a visit to the inflatable first-aider, the inflatable boy and the inflatable teacher were repaired, but the entire school was now in a great airless heap on the floor.

The inflatable headmaster called the inflatable boy to what remained of his office. 'I hope you're ashamed of yourself,' the headmaster said crossly. 'You've let the school down. You've let your teacher down. But worst of all, you've let yourself down.'

CHAPTER 5
SPOOF STUFF

THE DEADLIEST JOKES EVER
by Di Laffing

THE SURVIVORS' GUIDE
TO ESCAPING FROM A SINKING SHIP
by Mandy Lifeboats

DISASTER AT SEA!
By May Day

THAT'S JUST NOT FUNNY ANY MORE
by Bjorn de Joke

TATTY OLD FURNITURE
by Anne Teak

HOW TO THINK REALLY DEEPLY
by Phil Ossofy

GONE FISHING
by Courtney Biggins

THE DIZZIEST DANCES OF ALL TIME
by Ed Banger

SPOOF STUFF

STINKING RICH
by Iona Castle

KEEPING NASTY SMELLS AT BAY
by Lydia Dustbin

THE FINAL ACT
by Kurt N Call

THE PERFECT ACCOMPANIMENT TO A CUP OF TEA
by Duncan Biskit

THE UNWANTED GUEST by Al B Back

A COMPLETE HISTORY OF MANMADE FABRICS by Polly S Terr

TOP TIPS FOR CHRISTMAS KISSES by Miss L Tow

MY DAD'S LOST HIS CAR KEYS AGAIN by Fran Tick

SPOOF STUFF

THE GOOD FOOD GUIDE FOR DOGS
by Nora Bone

Sliding Down the Bannister
by Major Bumsore

HOW TO KEEP YOUR HALL TIDY
by Angus McCoatupp

I GIVE UP
by Sir N Derr

NEVER GIVE UP by Percy Vere

ALL THE FUN OF THE FAIR by Tom Bowler

THE GIRL WHO COULDN'T STOP COMPLAINING by Mona Lott

THE PROS AND CONS OF FIGHTING by Warren Peas

SPOOF STUFF

WHAT MAKES LIGHTBULBS GLOW? by Elektra City

THE MOST POPULAR CHINESE DISHES OF ALL TIME by Chris P Duck

THE POLITE POLICEMEN by Eve Ninall

THE GENEROUS MILLIONAIRE by Benny Factor

IS THERE LIFE ON MARS?
by Howard I. No

THE AMAZING VANISHING WOMAN
by Fay de Way

THE ROMAN WHO WAS SACKED FROM HIS CONSTRUCTION JOB
by Ben Dinroad

PERFECT PLACE TO KEEP ALL YOUR PANTS
by Chester Drawers

SPOOF STUFF

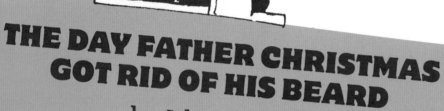

THE DAY FATHER CHRISTMAS GOT RID OF HIS BEARD
by Klaus Shave

THE MAN WHO COULDN'T STOP
by Juan Moore-Thyme

HOW TO KEEP A HOUSE WARM IN WINTER
by Ray D. A. Torr

WHAT TO DO WHEN THE SAND'S TOO HOT TO WALK ON
by Lee Ping

I LOVE TO SING EXTREMELY LOUDLY AND SLIGHTLY OFF-KEY IN PUBLIC
by Carrie Oakey

PUTTING ONE BRICK ON TOP OF ANOTHER IN A REALLY NEAT WAY
by Bill Ding

THE SECRET OF MEGA-SPEEDY COOKERY
by Mike Rowave

HOW TO FIT A SAFETY NET
by Justin Case

SPOOF STUFF

JANE AIR

The Nineteenth-Century
Romantic Heroine who
Suffered from Terrible Wind

WAR AND PEAS

The Battle of the Small
Green Vegetables

GRIMM'S FURRY TALES
or Cute and Cuddly Classics

THE SWORD IN THE SCONE
or When King Arthur Discovered that he Needed Contact Lenses

CHARLOTTE'S WORLD WIDE WEB
or The Spider Who got Broadband

JUST SEW STORIES
A Collection of Needlework and Embroidery Fables

JAMES AND THE GIANT PITCH
A Marvellous Football Fable

SPOOF STUFF

THE WONDERFUL WIZARD OF OZ
or The Fantastic Magician from Down Under

LITTLE RED RIDING HOOD
or The Coat that Shrank in the Wash

THE NIGHT BEFORE CHRISTMAS
or What Happened on the Twenty Forth of December

FIVE CHILDREN AND IT
or A Group of Kids Learn Computer Skills

LITTLE WOMEN
or Four Sisters All Under Five Feet Tall

THE JUNGLE BOOK
or Survival Tips for Young Explorers

THE CAT IN THE HAT
or The Magician who Misplaced his Rabbit

WHERE THE WILD THINGS ARE
or Check Under Your Bed Before you go to Sleep

SPOOF STUFF

HARRY POTTER AND THE GOBLET OF CLAY
One boy's mission to master the art of pottery

NANNY MCPHEE-EW
The story of a Scottish nanny who ran a marathon

MONSTERS' INK
Monsters' pens don't work without it

SCOOBY DON'T
The story of a dog who never has any adventures

51 DALMATIONS
The abridged version

THE SOUND OF MOOSIC

A bovine epic, featuring the most melodic cows in Austria

THE JINGLE BOOK

A Christmassy film of sleighbells

DOCTOR DOLOTSANDLOTS

The man who wouldn't stop talking to the animals, even when they REALLY wanted him to shut up

SPOOF STUFF

STAR WARS
The battle of the TV celebrities

GREASE
A sticky tale of solidified chip fat

JURASSIC PARK
One palaeontologist's historic discovery of a prehistoric playground

THE POLAR EXPRESS
The story of the number-one Arctic newspaper

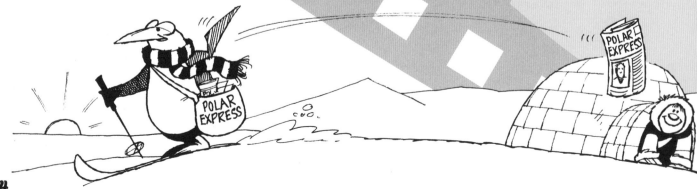

WHAT THE FILM WAS REALLY ABOUT

LOSING NEMO
Oops, there he goes again

ALICE IN SUNDERLAND
Alice takes a trip to the north-east of England

STINKERBELL
The naughtiest - and smelliest - fairy ever

NICE AGE
A bunch of prehistoric creatures have a lovely time, with no trouble at all from snow, ice or predators

DOWN
The eagerly awaited sequel to 'Up'

SPOOF STUFF

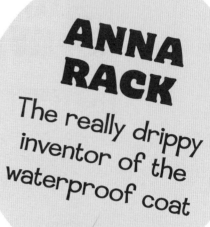

MEGAN STUFFUP

The fairytale writer

NOAH ZARK

The number-one shipbuilder

LAURA NORDER

The policewoman who arrested the most people ever

XL ENTMARKS

The best exam-passer ever

LOU POLE

The world-class barrister

GOLDi-SHOCKS!

Goldilocks was taking a stroll one lovely, sunny afternoon when she came across a charming house hidden in the middle of the woods. A warm, inviting cooking smell was wafting out of the open door.

Suddenly Goldilocks felt really hungry! So she crept in, her nose following the sweet smell. There were three bowls of porridge on the table. 'Hello? Anyone home?' she called out, but no one answered.

Her tummy rumbled noisily, so Goldilocks sat down at the table and took a mouthful from the first bowl. 'Ouch!' she exclaimed, it was too hot, so she tried the second bowl. 'Yuk!' she cried, it was too cold, so she tried the third bowl. 'Mmm...' this porridge was just right.

Yummy, sweet and delicious.

Goldilocks gulped down the whole lot and licked the bowl clean. After that she felt really, really tired. Letting out a big yawn, she got up and searched for a bed so she could have a nap. She looked in all the rooms on the bottom floor, but found nothing, so she went up the stairs, feeling really sleepy.

She went into the first room, 'At last!' she said, as she dived onto the big bed.

'Ow!' shouted Goldilocks, the bed was too hard, so she went into the second room where she found another bed, which she hopped into. 'Oh no' said sleepy Goldilocks, it was much too soft, so dragging her feet, she went into the third room where she immediately screamed in surprise! Inside were three little pigs, all staring at her.

'What are you three doing here?' said Goldilocks, 'You're in the wrong fairy tale!'

'No we're not,' answered one of the pigs. 'This is a two-story house.'

CHAPTER 6
TOTALLY POTTY

Why did Tigger peer down the toilet?

He was looking for Pooh.

What do polar bears get when they sit on the ice for too long?

Polaroids.

How many windy schoolboys does it take to stink out a gymnasium?

A phew.

Which famous bear loved to sit on the loo?

Winnie the Pooh.

What's got a bottom at the top?

A toilet.

How do you make a toilet roll?

Push it down a slope.

What did one toilet say to the other toilet?

You look flushed.

Q. Did you hear about the dastardly thieves who stole all the toilets from the police station?

A. Detectives have nothing to go on.

TOTALLY POTTY

Why did the sleepy boy
do laps of his bed?

He wanted to catch up
on his sleep.

Where do forgetful
parrots live?

Polynesia.

What's the difference
between a boy
and a dog?

A boy wears
trousers and
a dog just pants.

What tree
never grows?

A lava tree.

Q: DID YOU HEAR ABOUT THE HARD-WORKING PLUMBER?

Why couldn't the girl daydream? Her mind kept wandering.

Why did the peach go out with the raisin?

Because he couldn't find a date!

What type of joke does a clever duck tell?

A wise quack.

Where do young cows go for their lunch?

A calfeteria.

TOTALLY POTTY

Why did the Victorian holidaymaker float?

His trunks were made of wood.

What does a table-tennis table smell like?

It has a terrible ping-pong.

What did the seaweed say when it got stuck in the rock pool?

Kelp! Kelp!

What do you call a girl who stands in the sea and lets people walk all over her?

Pia.

When's the best time to dive into a swimming pool?

When there's water in it.

What did the dancer with two left feet wear to the holiday disco?

Flip-flips.

Why did the holidaymakers smell of salt and pepper?

They were seasoned travellers.

What dries as it gets wetter?

A towel.

TOTALLY POTTY

Did you hear about the stick of rock that was hard of hearing?

It was stone deaf.

What do you call a man-made Greek holiday island? Con-Crete.

What's the sweetest type of music you get beside the seaside?

Rock.

What did the wave say to the sea?

It's high tide I got out of here.

What do pickpockets do when they spot the police at the funfair?

Dodgem.

What was the hairdresser's favourite funfair ride?

The roller coaster.

What do you call an ice cream man with a 99 in one ear and an ice lolly in the other?

Anything you like, he can't hear you.

What was the ballroom dancer's favourite funfair ride?

The waltzer.

TOTALLY POTTY

How much did the American pirate pay to get his ears pierced?

A buck an ear.

Why did the orange go to the doctor?

He wasn't peeling too well.

Why was it so easy for Sherlock Holmes to learn his ABCs?

Because it was LMN-try.

What did the Scuba diver say to the ship?

I can see your bottom.

What do martial arts experts cook on the barbeque?

Karate chops.

Why did the King go to the dentist?

To get his teeth crowned!

Which dinosaur has to shelter from the rain?

A Stegosau-rust.

What does a Triceratops sit on?

Its Tricera-bottom.

TOTALLY POTTY

What is the one vegetable that you should never ever take on a boat?

A leek.

What did one snowman say to the other snowman?

Smells like carrots.

Why was the painting sent to prison?

Because it was framed.

What goes out but never comes in?

A candle.

Which type of tree is invited to the most parties?

The Poplar tree.

What can you catch but never throw?

A cold.

What is hard to beat?

A bongo drum with a hole in it.

Can a jam jar dance?

No, but a tin can can!

TOTALLY POTTY

What do you get if you cross a fairytale character and a large, grey animal with huge ears and a trunk?

Cinderellaphant.

What do you get if you divide the circumference of a pumpkin by its diameter?

Pumpkin pi.

What is the fruitiest lesson?

History, because it's full of dates.

What did the boy scout say after he fixed the horn on the toy car?

Beep repaired!

What did one ice cream seller say to the other ice cream seller?

Have an ice day!

What did the two famous composers take to the supermarket with them?

A Chopin Liszt.

What's the difference between roast beef and pea soup?

You can roast beef.

Q. What do you get if you cross a fairytale character and a treasure chest?

A. **Sleeping Booty.**

TOTALLY POTTY

What do you call a large rectangle of wood with nothing to do?

Board.

Why did the orange stop rolling down the slope?

It didn't have any juice left.

A pizza walks into a bar and asks for a roast dinner.
'I'm sorry,' says the barman

'We don't serve food.'

What do you call a Tyrannosaurus rex stuck in quicksand?

Anything you like, he can't chase you.

What do you get if you cross a fairytale character and a pharmacy?

Puss in Boots.

What do you call an alien with five eyes?

Aliiiiien.

If Martians live on Mars and Venutians live on Venus and Saturnians live on Saturn, who lives on Pluto?

Fleas.

TOTALLY POTTY

William Shakespeare
walks into a cafe.

'Hey, you!' shouts the
waiter. 'You're Bard!'

What's green
and hard?

A frog
in boxing
gloves.

What's tall, grey, spiky
and runs around
a prison?

The prison wall.

Q: WHAT'S THE SCARIEST CONFECTIONARY OF ALL?

Why couldn't the girl have a dog for Christmas?

Because her mum said they were having a turkey like every other year.

What did the fish say when it swam into a concrete wall?

Dam.

Did you hear about the boy who went to buy a camouflage jacket?

He couldn't find one.

What happened when the dog kennels went bust?

They called in the retrievers.

What do you get if you cross a bird with a breakfast cereal?

Shredded Tweet.

TOTALLY POTTY

When is a racing car
not a racing car?
When it turns into
a pit lane.

Did you hear about
the fish who couldn't
stop complaining?
**He liked
to carp.**

Which dinosaurs
lie about on the
seashore?

Tyrannosaurus-
wrecks.

What's black and white
and black and white
and black and white?
A penguin rolling
down a hill.

Where is Captain Hook's treasure chest?

In his treasure shirt.

What do you say to a pole vaulter?

Hiya!

Did you hear about the boy who had to visit the doctor after swallowing all of his pocket money?

There's no change yet.

On which day of the year does a cow get a bunch of flowers and breakfast in bed?

Mudders Day.

TOTALLY POTTY

Q. Why did the bald man sit a rabbit on his head?

A. From a distance, they look like hares.

What's the cleverest car in the world?
A Smart car.

What type of pants do storm clouds wear?
Thunderpants!

Did you hear about the man who fell over in the Indian restaurant?
He slipped into a korma.

Did you hear about the fight at the fish'n'chip shop?

Two fish were battered.

What did the rug say to the wooden floor?

Don't worry. I've got you covered.

What sound does a steam train make when it has a cold?

Aaaaah-choo-choo!

Where do milkshakes come from?

Riverdancing cows.

TOTALLY POTTY

Why did the cricket captain hire a new chef?

He needed a good batter.

What do you call a flying police officer?

A helicopper.

What do you get if you cross a kangaroo and a toilet?

A kangaloo.

What did the egg say to the electric whisk?

I know when I'm beaten.

Why did the carrot look down the toilet?

He wondered where the peas had gone.

How do ancient Egyptian monarchs travel?

By Pharaoh-plane.

Q. Why did the farmer bury his money instead of putting it in the bank?

A. He wanted to make his soil richer.

Which dog uses a punchbag?

A boxer.

A BUG'S LIFE

But as the weevils grew up, they went their separate ways.

One weevil became a champion eater. He gobbled everything that the local farmer grew, munching his way through meadow after meadow of delicious crops. And when he'd finished, he moved on to the next farm and the one after that.

The bigger he became, the more he ate. In the world of weevils, he became very famous indeed. In fact, he was a celebrity weevil.

The other weevil was more of a picky eater. He looked for the tastiest ears of corn and rejected the rest, so he never grew big or famous. And he definitely wasn't a celebrity.

Once there was a pair of young weevils. The little insects were the best of friends and did everything together – they played together, nibbled the local farmer's crops together and laughed at each other's silly jokes, (which were very silly indeed).

One day, a weevil TV crew decided to make a documentary of the celebrity weevil's life story. They came to interview the unknown weevil and asked all about his old friend. 'That's interesting,' said the weevil interviewer when they'd heard all about the celebrity weevil's early years.

'I have just one last question. Why is it that you never hit the big time? You've never destroyed an entire crop in your whole life.'

'Well,' said the insect. 'I'm the lesser of two weevils, you see.'

CHAPTER 7
TOO SILLY FOR WORDS

Why was the pasta kept in the collander?

There was a restraining order.

What do you call an overweight pumpkin?

A plumpkin.

What goes putt-putt-putt-putt-putt?

A dreadful golfer.

If the orange house is on the left side of the street and the purple house is on the right side of the street, where is the white house?

Washington, DC.

Did you hear about the man who didn't use the letters E, F, O, R or T?
He couldn't spell for toffee.

If you get an umpire in cricket and a referee in football, what do you get in bowls?
Fruit.

What's conjunctivitis.com?
It's a site for sore eyes.

What do you get if you cross Batman and Robin with a steamroller?
Flatman and Ribbon.

TOO SILLY FOR WORDS

Q. Which fruit once ruled the world?

A. Alexander the Grape.

What kind
of scones do
pilots prefer?

Plain.

What kind of meal do
climbers eat on top
of a mountain?

High tea.

Which month
has 28 days?

All of them!

Big brother: If this planet is Mars, what's that one?
Little brother: Pa's.

Did you hear about the bad-tempered boy who lost one shoe?

He was hopping mad.

Did you hear about the French chef who was a champion first-aider too?

He gave patients the quiche of life.

What did the two-storey house say to the one-storey house?
Bung-allo-allo-allo.

TOO SILLY FOR WORDS

What's the hardest thing about learning to ride a bicycle?

The ground.

How do you teach a baby car to drive properly?

Work on its motor skills.

Why didn't the girl go straight home from school?

Because she lived around the corner.

Which tables don't they teach you in Maths?

Dinner tables.

What do Norwegians drive? Fjord Mustangs.

What was Camelot? The place where King Arthur's Eyptian friends parked their camels.

Which computer will keep you dry in the rain? A Mac.

Did the secretary file her nails? No, just the paperwork.

TOO SILLY FOR WORDS

Did you hear about the criminal wearing a camouflage suit whose shoelaces were tied together?

He could hide but he couldn't run.

If two wrongs don't make a right, what does? Three lefts.

Did you hear about the little old lady on the zebra crossing with super-human strength?

She could hold up traffic.

Why does the statue of Nelson stand on top of Nelson's column?

Because it can't sit down.

Did you hear about the girl who was bopped on the head by the frisbee?

She wondered why it was getting bigger and then it hit her.

Did you hear about the unemployed court jester?

He was no one's fool.

What happened when the boy with no jokes announced he was going to be a stand-up comedian?

Everybody laughed.

Why are oil rig workers so sleepy?

Because drilling for oil is boring.

TOO SILLY FOR WORDS

Why didn't the top salon stylist cut hair any longer?

Because she cut it shorter.

What do you call an incredibly polite person who builds bridges and lays roads?

A civil engineer.

Where do you find a giant scholar?

Around the neck of a giant's shirt.

Where do you make all-singing and all-dancing Xs?

In an X-Factory.

Why did the target run away just before the archery contest began?

It wanted to make an arrow escape.

Where do candles go to learn to be celebrity popstars?

Flame Academy.

Who was the toughest, most ruthless sea creature ever?

Billy the Squid.

In a family with seven children, why was the youngest late for school?

The alarm was only set for six.

TOO SiLLY FOR WORDS

Did you hear about the letter O that kept gnashing its teeth?

It was a vicious circle.

Why did Robinson Crusoe say 'Goodbye' on Thursday?

Because he was leaving Friday.

When is an exam paper not an exam paper?

When it's turned in to the examiner.

Why does a tricycle stand up on its own?

Because it isn't too tired.

Q: WHY DID THE OWNER OF THE CAKE SHOP LAUGH?

What's the capital of Iceland?

I.

Which king had a numb bottom?

The one who was longest on the throne.

Where do cows go on holiday?

Moo York!

What did one Arctic explorer say to the other Arctic explorer?

I'd hate to have a bear behind in this weather.

TOO SILLY FOR WORDS

Did you hear about the man who parked his car in a tow-away zone?

When he got back, the whole street was gone.

Why wouldn't the bald man lend anyone his comb?

He couldn't part with it.

Are thieves right-handed or left-handed?
Neither. They're red-handed.

Why do magicians have such dainty fingers?

Because they're sleight-of-hand.

Did you hear about the boy who spilt Spot remover on his dog?

The dog vanished.

What did the watermelon say to the avocado?

Nothing. Watermelons can't talk.

What's the quickest way to make a fire with two sticks?

When one of them is a match.

Q. Why couldn't anyone telephone the zoo?

A. Because the lion was busy.

TOO SILLY FOR WORDS

Why couldn't anyone telephone the bride-to-be?

Because she was engaged.

What starts with P and ends with E and has thousands of letters in it?

Post Office.

What did the television order from the takeaway?

The satellite dish.

What do you call a herb that draws pictures?

Dill-ustrator!

Why couldn't the sailor's knot and the angler's knot go ashore and have some fun? **They were all tied up.**

What does a greengrocer who is six feet tall weigh? **Vegetables.**

What was Robin Hood's mum called? **Mother Hood.**

Why did the girl spray her alarm clock with insect repellent? **It was full of ticks.**

TOO SILLY FOR WORDS

Why couldn't anyone telephone the launderette?

Because there was nothing on the line.

What can you serve, but never eat?

A tennis ball.

What kind of vehicle gets the hiccups?

A hiccup truck.

Q. How does Jack Frost travel?

A. By icicle.

Did you hear about the doctor who looked at the empty waiting room and got really really cross?

She had no patients.

Where do ice cream sellers learn how to make ice cream?

At sundae school.

Which miserable painting is never ever happy?

The Moaning Lisa.

What does a clock have after eating?

Seconds.

TOO SILLY FOR WORDS

Why couldn't Batman go fishing?

Because Robin had eaten all the worms.

Which ancient king invented the fireplace?

Alfred the Grate.

What do you call a very short fortune-teller who is on the run from the police?

A small medium at large.

Why couldn't the car play football?

Because it only had one boot.

What did one maths textbook say to the other maths textbook?

I've got problems.

Why do businesspeople carry umbrellas?

Because umbrellas can't walk.

Did you hear about the man who ate a lightbulb?

He fancied a light meal.

How did the cheeseburger propose?

With an onion ring.

TOO SILLY FOR WORDS

Why were the corduroy pillows in the news?

They made headlines.

Why did King Kong buy 20 pairs of shoes?

Because he was a 40-foot monster.

Why did the bank manager put the grandfather clock under his desk?

He wanted to work overtime.

What kind of a wig can hear?

An earwig.

Did you hear about the dim glowworm? He wasn't very bright.

What do you do with a green monster?

Wait until it ripens.

Did you hear about the really hot street corner?

It was 90 degrees.

Teacher:
Can you think of a sentence using the word 'fascinate'?

Pupil:
My grandad has a shirt with ten buttons down the front, but he has such a big tummy that he can only fascinate (fasten eight – geddit?!).

TOO SiLLY FOR WORDS

What's the laziest
type of shoe?

A loafer.

What did Picasso
eat for breakfast?

Surreal.

Did you hear about
the thief who stole
the camp bed?

He's been
lying low.

Did you hear about
the string section of the orchestra
that held up the bank?

It was robbery with violins.

Is it a good idea to swim on a full stomach?

No. It's much better to go to a swimming pool.

What do lawyers wear on their feet? Court shoes.

When things go horribly wrong and you've been let down by everyone and everything, what can you always count on?

Your fingers.

Q. What's the fittest type of shoe?

A. A trainer.

THRONES AND GROANS

could afford was grass, but they did their best and wove the king a truly magnificent grass castle with turrets and a drawbridge and a fantastic grass throne.

Once upon a time, there was a king. He was poor and the people who lived in his kingdom were poor. But the king was a jolly nice king, who told jokes, held parties and helped his people as much as he could by abolishing taxes.

One day the king's loyal subjects decided to build the king a new castle to say thank you for being so wonderful. They were so poor that the only building material they

The country next door was much richer than the first country and they laughed when they saw the grass castle with its grass drawbridge and grass throne. 'You can't sit on that!' said the neighbouring king. 'Here, have my old wooden throne. It's much more royal-looking.'

'Okey doke,' said the king. But secretly, he preferred his own throne and he popped the big wooden one in the grass loft of his grass castle and then went to sit on the grass throne instead.

But the wooden throne was so heavy that it broke through the grass floor of the loft, plummeted down and fell on the king's head, squashing him flat. Oops.

'Hmm,' said one of the king's people.

'People who live in grass houses shouldn't stow thrones.'

CRASH!

CHAPTER 8
WILLY-NILLY SILLY

I'm reading this book called
"*A History of Glue*".
I can't put it down!

What's the name of a book
that tells the life story
of a car?
An autobiography.

What's taller
than a giant?
A giant's hat.

I'm reading another book called
"*Nuts and Bolts*".
It's riveting.

What did the 8 say to the 3?

Where's your other half?

What lies at the bottom of the sea and shivers?

A nervous wreck.

Why did the boy keep his guitar in the fridge?

Because he liked cool music.

How do dairy farmers add up?

On a cowculator.

WILLY-NILLY SILLY

What do you get if you cross a cobra trainer and a playwright?

William Snakespeare.

A cowboy rode to the Wild West Hotel on Friday. He stayed three nights and he left on Friday. How?

His horse was called Friday.

Which word in the dictionary is always spelt wrongly? **Wrongly.**

What do you get if you cross a Roman emperor with a lettuce and a tomato?

Caesar salad.

Why did the atoms say goodbye?
It was time to split.

What's the best way to keep a total idiot busy for hours and hours and hours?

Give him a piece of paper with 'please turn over' written on both sides.

Did you hear about the martial-arts specialist with a bad cold?

It was kung flu.

Did you hear about the strawberry who attended charm school?

He became a real fruit smoothie.

WiLLY-NiLLY SiLLY

How did the witch keep her broomstick safe?

With a warlock.

How did the hermit cover his rent and bills?

Alone.

Why did the break dancer buy a car?

He fancied taking it for a spin.

Where do snowmen dance?

At snowballs.

When is the best time to eat fresh asparagus?

When you're hungry.

What did the jack say to the broken-down car?

Can I give you a lift?

What's the name of a country where every single car is pink?

A pink car-nation.

How do you know when a weaver is telling you a fib?

They spin you a yarn.

WILLY-NILLY SILLY

Did you see the picture of the dangerous and deadly Lone Teddy Bear that was plastered all over the Wild West?

They were wan-ted posters.

HAVE YOU SEEN HIM?

How do dinosaurs pass their exams?

With extinction.

Where do burgers dance?

At meatballs.

What did the mother steam train say to the baby steam train at teatime?

Choo choo!

Why did the burger refuse to star in a blockbuster movie?

The roll wasn't good enough.

Did you hear about Mr Coles the scientist who sliced cabbage very thinly, added carrot, onion, a sprinkling of raisins and a dollop of mayonnaise?

He invented Cole's Law.

Did you hear about the neutron who took a trolley full of shopping to the checkout?

There was no charge.

Why did the maths teacher tell her student that he was average.

She was being mean.

WILLY-NILLY SILLY

Did you hear about
the quad babies?

**Four crying
out loud.**

Why did the
potato cry?

**Its peelings
were hurt.**

What's the best way
to catch a train?

Follow its tracks.

What did one gooseberry
say to the other
gooseberry?

**If you hadn't been
so juicy, we wouldn't
be in this jam.**

Where do cars cry?

On the hard shoulder.

A: A TEDDY BRRRRR

Why did the girl wear banana skins on her feet? **She'd lost her slippers.**

Did you hear about the jolly fortune teller who wasn't too big and wasn't too small?

She was a happy medium.

Q. Why is an island like the letter T?

A. **They're both in the middle of water.**

WiLLY-NiLLY SiLLY

What did the letter
say to the stamp?
**Stick with me and
we'll go places.**

What do you call a
line of Barbie dolls?
A barbeque.

Did you hear about the man who found
a note on his windscreen complimenting
him on his driving skills?
It said, 'Parking fine'.

What's full of holes
and still holds water?
A sponge.

What has four eyes and can't see?
The Mississippi river.

Did you hear about the unemployed origami specialist?
His company folded.

How do you put a circus out of action?
Go for the juggler.

What's green, round and goes camping?
A boy sprout.

WILLY-NILLY SILLY

Which famous brothers didn't invent the aeroplane?

The Wrong brothers.

What do you get when you cross a film projector and a swimming pool?

A dive-in cinema.

Why did the man give his watch to the building society?

He wanted to save time.

How do you make a stiff drink?

Put cement in your cup.

Did you hear about the firework that was stopped by the police?

They let him off.

Why did the girl disappear into the bowl of muesli?

A strong currant pulled her under.

What is orange and sounds like a parrot?

A carrot.

Q. Did you hear about the crowd of bank robbers that rushed into the sea?

A. **They started a crime wave.**

WiLLY-NiLLY SiLLY

Who invented the match?
Some bright spark.

What do you
call a sleeping
Stegosaurus?
A dinosnore.

If two collars raced
each other,
how would it all end?

In a tie.

What language do
people speak in Cuba?

Cubic.

When do you need
a wombat?

When you're
playing a game
of wom.

How do you
make an
apple puff?

Chase it round
the park.

Why was the king so good
at drawing straight lines?

Because he
was a ruler.

Did you hear the
dreadful joke about the
pile of manure?

It stinks.

WILLY-NILLY SILLY

How did the lady marry sixteen people in one day?

She was a registrar.

Why did the weather forecaster look out of her window first thing every morning?

Because she couldn't see through the wall.

What does the queen do after she's burped?

She issues a royal pardon.

What exams do farmers take?

Hay Levels.

Why did the chicken sit on an axe?

She wanted to hatchet.

What do you get if you cross a caterpillar with a parrot?
A walkie-talkie.

Why did the book spy on people?
It was a peeping tome.

Q. Why was Cinderella so terrible at tennis?

A. She had a pumpkin for a coach.

WiLLY-NiLLY SiLLY

Customer:
Can I try on that dress in the window?

Shop assistant:
Certainly, madam. But we'd prefer it if you used the changing room.

Which two meals can you never have for breakfast?
Lunch and dinner.

Why did the explorer go to the South Pole?
To visit Aunt Arctica.

Did you hear about the apple crumble, rhubarb crumble and gooseberry crumble trial?

They all ended up in custardy.

What did the vegetarian Prime Minister dearly want to do?

Give peas a chance.

Did you hear about the comedian who told his audience he'd run out of gags?

He wasn't joking.

What do you call a deer with no eyes?

No idea.

Did you hear about the boy who dreamt he wrote *The Lord of the Rings*?

He was Tolkien in his sleep.

WILLY-NILLY SILLY

What do gardeners read when they're eating their packed lunch?

Weeder's Digest.

Did you hear about the bonkers golfer?

He was a crack putt.

What's green and jumps a lot?

A frog with hiccups.

What has 50 heads and 50 tails?

50 coins.

What goes, 'OH, OH, OH'?

Father Christmas walking backwards.

What's the richest kind of air?

A gazillionaire.

What do you get if you cross a satsuma with a stand-up comedian?

Peels of laughter.

What did the big broom say to the little broom?

It's time to go to sweep.

WiLLY-NiLLY SiLLY

Why is it very tricky to open a piano?

All the keys are inside.

Why was the bass guitarist arrested? He got in treble.

What do horses watch to relax?

Saddle-lite TV.

How do Swedish people dress in winter?

Quickly.

How do you turn a watch into a stopwatch?

Don't wind it.

What is red and yellow and pink and green and orange and purple and blue and black and white and brown?

A box of colouring pencils.

How do you make golden soup?

With eighteen carrots.

Q. What did one Venus fly trap say to the other Venus fly trap?

A. Time's fun when you're having flies.

WiLLY-NiLLY SiLLY

What do you call a man who's covered in cat scratches?

Claude.

What did the snake say to his girlfriend after an argument?

Let's hiss and make up!

How do you make an onion giggle?
Pickle it!

How did Noah see the animals on the ark at night?
He used flood lighting.

What are fortune tellers' favourite plants?
Palm trees!

Why did the toadstool move house?
It didn't have mushroom.

Why are skunks so obedient?
Because they go wherever they're scent.

What do you call a really spoilt cat?
Pam Purred.

BUGGED

A girl is on her way to school when an enormous stag beetle jumps onto the pavement in front of her. 'Ner-ner-ner-ner-ner!' it shouts. 'You smell!'

The girl watches as the stag beetle scuttles off. 'That wasn't very nice.' she says to herself and carries on towards school.

When she gets there, everyone is talking about the huge insect. 'It told me I was fat!' says one boy. 'It called me specky-four-eyes!' says another. 'Pay no attention.' says the teacher.

On the way home from school, the girl keeps a lookout for the stag beetle. She has no desire to be insulted again. But the beetle finds her – and this time it calls her 'a blithering idiot' and then throws a water balloon at her. The girl is drenched with water and so upset that when she gets home, her mother decides to take her to see the doctor.

The doctor listens to everything, occasionally nods his head and at last he speaks.

'Hmmm,' he says. 'I did hear that there was a nasty bug going around.'